AF593781

Paramahansa Yogananda
(1893–1952)

How to Change Others

by
Sri Daya Mata

"How-to-Live" Series
No. 1979

A publication of
SELF-REALIZATION FELLOWSHIP
Founded in 1920 by Paramahansa Yogananda

About the "How-to-Live" Series: These informal talks and essays were originally published by Self-Realization Fellowship in its quarterly magazine, *Self-Realization*. Some have also appeared in anthologies and on audiocassette recordings produced by the society. The "How-to-Live" series was created in response to requests from readers for pocket-size booklets presenting Paramahansa Yogananda's teachings on various subjects. The series offers guidance by Sri Yogananda and some of his longtime disciples, members of the monastic Self-Realization Order, many of whom had the opportunity to receive the spiritual direction and training of this beloved world teacher over a period of many years. New titles are added to the series periodically.

Authorized by the International Publications Council of
SELF-REALIZATION FELLOWSHIP
3880 San Rafael Avenue • Los Angeles, CA 90065-3298

Self-Realization Fellowship was founded by Paramahansa Yogananda as the instrument for the worldwide dissemination of his teachings. The Self-Realization Fellowship name and emblem (shown above) appear on all SRF books, recordings, and other publications, assuring the reader that a work originates with the society established by Paramahansa Yogananda and faithfully conveys his teachings.

~ *Second Printing, 1995* ~
Reprinted from *Only Love*

ISBN 0-87612-412-0
Printed in the United States of America on recycled paper
11609-54321

– ✧ –

There is a Power that will light your way to health, happiness, peace, and success, if you will but turn toward that Light.

—Paramahansa Yogananda

– ✧ –

How to Change Others

By Sri Daya Mata

Condensed from a talk given at the Self-Realization Fellowship India Hall Hollywood, California, May 19, 1965

The behavior of others should not be allowed to rob us of our peace of mind. It is difficult for anyone to remain mentally calm and hold his tongue when he is irritated by others, but no human being can successfully go through life telling everyone who annoys him how to behave. Unsolicited counsel creates tremendous resentment. One should not try to impose his will or ideas upon those around him unless they have asked for such guidance.

One mistake often made by novices on the spiritual path is that the moment they feel enthusiasm for seeking God, they want to change the whole world. They start a spiritual revolution in the home, with an all-out effort to convert the husband or wife and the children. It is wonderful to have that kind of eagerness, but it almost always arouses antagonism. Paramahansaji* used to say to such enthusiasts, "Change yourself first; reform yourself and you will reform thousands." Unless one is seeking guidance, he doesn't want to be told what to do. No one likes to have advice forced upon him. When he is ready for counsel he will ask for it, and he will want it from one with whom he lives, or whom he loves or admires, if he sees a beneficial change has taken place in that person's life. But so long as change is shown only in the form of platitudes or lip service, the doubter will resist.

Be an example of what you want others to be. If you are inclined to lose your temper and fight back or speak harshly; if you scold the children unreasonably; if you are nervous and easily upset, shouting and speaking unkindly—change yourself! That is the best way to change those around you. It is hard

* "Ji" is a respectful suffix added to names and titles in India.

to do, but it can be done. One's effort should be directed toward making himself a person who is respected and looked up to; whose word carries weight. He should speak from true wisdom and understanding, never from anger, nervousness, jealousy, or desire to retaliate when hurt.

In India, a very successful manufacturer came to me and said, "I am discouraged and upset; I am having trouble with my wife and with my employees. I am always speaking harsh words to them. What am I to do?"

"Do you want the truth, or do you want me to say what you hope to hear?"

"I want the truth."

"All right," I answered, "you have to begin with yourself. You have a reputation as a tyrant in your home and with your employees. As a result, others obey you because you hold a whip over them rather than because they love or respect you. Consequently you do not get from them the work or cooperation that you could. You should learn to let go;

stop being so tense. Every day take a little time to relax; take a little time to think about God. Pretend that in the next instant your whole life will be snuffed away, or pretend you are already dead." (It is a most interesting experiment. Suddenly you find that all your responsibilities are no longer yours. You realize how important it is to be more than a little bit concerned about your future with God.)

Then I said to him, "If you wish, while I am here, come every afternoon for *satsanga** and meditate with us." He came every day and we meditated and talked about God.

Two years later, when I was again in India, one of his employees told me, "He is a different man; so much calmer and more patient with us. Because of this there is more peace and harmony among us; we get

* Literally, "fellowship with truth." A *satsanga* is usually an informal gathering of truth-seekers at which the leader speaks extemporaneously about God and other spiritual subjects.

more done because we are not tense and nervous all the time." This is a wonderful example of what our Guru* teaches on this path of Self-Realization Fellowship.

So long as you show nervousness and tension around your husband or wife or children, they will react and behave in a similar way. It can't be otherwise. So if you want a different atmosphere in your home, you have to take the initiative. Do not expect an overnight change in your family. That seldom happens; change is a slow, natural process. And even if it never comes, do not be discouraged or overly concerned. Guruji used to say to us, "God gave every human being a blessed gift: the privacy of his own thoughts. Therein he can live and silently create a companionship and understanding with God that will gradually begin to reflect in his entire life—including his relationships with his family, his community, his world." Even if those around you do not change perceptibly, the

* See *guru* in glossary.

change that is wrought within yourself makes you less vulnerable to the misbehavior of others.

Who Is Responsible for Teenage Behavior?

Often I am approached by parents disconcerted by the ever widening "generation gap" between them and their children. There are many reasons for the problems of today's youth—taken together, these problems constitute a vast and complex subject. Metaphysically, there is the influence of karma, of past-life* experiences, in these reincarnated youths, which may be rooted in the tragedies of the wars, riots, and racial abuses of the past thirty years. There is also the effect of mass media. Each segment of society finds every other segment in its own living room on the television screen, and as our *paramguru,*† Swami Sri Yukteswar, said, "Company is stronger than will power."

* See *karma* and *reincarnation* in glossary.

† The guru of one's guru.

Consider also the general permissiveness of our society and the lowering of religious and moral standards, as evidenced in publications and entertainment. That which feeds the baser instincts in man is bound to bring out the crude animalistic qualities in him. But setting aside these broader considerations, let me dwell on a few basic truths about the parent-child relationship.

We should not wholly blame the teenagers for getting into the difficulties in which so many of them find themselves today. We should look to their parents, and the parents' parents. First and foremost, the parents themselves are frequently undisciplined, and therefore fail to set a good example. I don't mean a holier-than-thou example, but the right kind of example—of understanding, with firmness when firmness is necessary, but never disciplining when their own emotions are out of control. If a parent tries to understand his children he will not hide behind the attitude that "because I am your father (or mother) you have to obey me." That will not work with children.

In addition to giving them love, parents should learn to be companions to their little ones, and this relationship should start at an early age. If parents do not cultivate a rapport with their children when the latter are still very young, there will be no parent-child communication as the youngsters grow older.

Children should not be overindulged with gifts in an attempt to satisfy all their desires. They should have to work for some of the things they want so they will know and appreciate their value. If they do not learn this at home, life will teach it to them sooner or later, perhaps under unfortunate circumstances. Children should be taught to feel a responsibility to earn and merit what they receive.

In some homes the mother does all the cooking, all the dishes, all the housework, and the children are given no duties or responsibilities. This is not right. Children should be expected to perform little chores within their capabilities and age limit. Each should be taught a sense of responsibility and self-respect as a rightful and contributing member of the family.

It is very important that parents understand the child's point of view, that they always try to see things as the child sees them. Then the parents can better help the child to see the matter correctly and in the right perspective. And never, never should the parent scold or spank a child when the parent is himself angry or emotional. The child will not respect or respond to that kind of discipline. He will respect the parent who behaves toward him with wisdom, love, and understanding.

Parents should think clearly and carefully before they lay down the law to their child, and then when they say "No," they must mean it. The child should not be allowed to feel that sooner or later his parents will forget what they said and he will then be able to do what he wants. Children are smarter than you may realize. They should not be given the opportunity to think that if they bide their time long enough one of the parents will relax his insistence on obedience. The child is clever enough to know what he can get away with; it is human nature.

The successful parent will always think first, "Is what I am going to say to my child a mere assertion of my own opinion and authority; or is it right because it is reasonable and just?" Then once having said it, he should make the child obey. A child will come to respect that kind of discipline if at the same time he sees it is meted out with fairness and understanding. His love and respect will make him want to try to please his worthy parent.

Today there is so much defiance in children. It is because they have never been taught that a part of life is learning to respect authority and the rights of others. How many parents, a few years ago, believed in the idea that a child is a young adult who should be allowed complete freedom of will to express himself. Good heavens! Why do you suppose God put parents here on earth? If He hadn't intended that children have the guidance of a mother and father, He would have had the parents lay eggs, so that once the children were hatched the parents could walk away and leave them to their own devices, as the turtle does. God expects parents to assume the responsibility of molding their offspring. Couples who bring a child into this world have no right to fail him.

I believe a child should be encouraged to go to Sunday school, but that he should never be compelled to do so. It is a mistake to try to force a child into any particular religious mold. First he has to have a desire for and an interest in things spiritual. This inclination will be there if from a very early age he is encouraged in cultivating spiritual attitudes: love for God, faith in God, a feeling of companionship with Him. Paramahansaji taught that there should be regular periods when parents and children come together for prayer and meditation. In this way the child begins to relate to God through the parents' example. But family worship should not be too long because children are restless and their minds are not controlled. It is difficult for them to sit long at one time. An excellent practice is to read or tell children stories that will develop in them a sense of morality, faith, right behavior, and love for God. This is the ideal of India. There the earliest instructions that reach the sensitive and receptive ears of the children are the noble and inspiring stories of the scriptures.

Children should never be given the impression that if they do wrong God is going to punish them. They must learn to love God, not to fear Him; to do right because they love Him. They should be taught a little bit about the karmic law: "What you sow in this world, my dears, you will also reap. If you tell lies, then others will be untruthful to you, and they will not trust you. If you steal or take forcibly from others, then others will also take from you. But if you are unselfish, others will be generous to you. If you are loving, others will love you."

It is the duty of parents to open up the minds and hearts of their children and to guide them in the cultivation of the right attitude toward life, toward their emotional problems, and toward sex, when they are old enough. While they are being taught, they should always feel that no matter what they do, their parents will always have an open heart and an understanding mind. A child ought not to feel that he has to go to someone else for the understanding he did not get from his parents.

A wise parent will never act astounded, overcome, dismayed, or shocked by anything his child says to him. The child should always be made to feel, "I can go to my mother and father with anything that is troubling me, because I know I will always receive understanding."

Once a youth came to me and said, "I can't talk to my father or mother. The moment I try to discuss my problems—and they are deep for me—my parents seem not to want to listen; or they scold me, or give me ultimatums. They won't allow me a chance to express myself; so as a result, I've learned to be quiet. I don't talk with them. They don't know these thoughts and these troubles I am having. They are too busy, or they don't want to hear them, or they are too impatient with me."

This is one of the great mistakes parents make; they do not take the time to identify with their children's problems and interests. Instead they reason, "Isn't it enough that I give you a home and see that you have good clothes, that I give you a car on Saturdays and let you go out with this one and that one, and that I give you so many of the things you want, including a vacation trip every year?" No, that is not enough. Those things will never take the place of understanding and companionship.

Every parent wants his children someday to say, "I am thankful for my parents; they were firm with me, but I always knew they loved me and that I could go to them with anything, knowing I would receive understanding, guidance, and patience." But in order to be that kind of mother or father, the parent must also be willing to discipline himself. He has to set the right example, physically, morally, intellectually, and spiritually. He has to cultivate wisdom, patience, and understanding, and he has to exercise perfect self-control whenever he is dealing with his child. Thus will he be able to fulfill the divine responsibility he takes upon himself when he brings a child into this world.

The Divine Meaning Behind Human Relationships

God gave us human relationships in various forms for one reason: we are to learn from one another. Everyone is in a sense our "guru," our teacher. Children teach us, they discipline us; we have to learn endless patience and how to reach out of ourselves, outside our own selfishness and self-interest, in order to help mold their lives correctly. We in turn are their "gurus," for it is our responsibility to guide and train them and give them the best possible start in life.

From all these relationships we acquire an expansion and purification of our love; and I believe that, in the ultimate sense, only love can change others. If you approach a child, or a husband, or anyone, in that consciousness of love and endless understanding no matter what they say or do, no matter how they hurt you, you can't help but win in the end. But you must also have the patience to go on trying.

Set the example in your own life of the qualities you want to bring out in others. "How to live"—that is a great science. Paramahansaji said to us, "When I went to my guru, Swami Sri Yukteswar, he told me,

'Learn to behave.'" And so must you learn to behave in this world: that is the science of religion. When you learn how to behave, you will know what God is, because you will then conduct yourself in such a manner that you will know every moment that you are the soul, not the mortal body or mind. The soul is always drinking deeply of the divine nectar of God's presence. You are not a mortal being, you are a divine being; so learn to behave like one.

That can only be done when a person puts religion into practical, everyday practice, as Self-Realization Fellowship teaches us. Religion isn't something to be gloriously expounded on Sundays and forgotten the rest of the week. Our Guru said to us, "I am not interested in ordinary church followers. If I were, I could have had thousands upon thousands throughout the world. I came to pick out of the crowds of searchers those souls who are deeply and sincerely in earnest about knowing God." He didn't mean that he wanted to make monastics of everyone. He used to say, "Make your heart a hermitage, where you can silently retire to worship God." In that hermitage of your heart put God first. How wonderful it is when He becomes the Beloved of your soul, the Friend of your soul, the Father, the Mother, the Companion, the Guru of your soul. Life becomes rewarding, your relationships with others joyous experiences. You love your children, your husband, your wife, with God's greater love and understanding and compassion. He strengthens the ties between human beings, between human hearts, and frees their earthly relationships from the bonds of selfish attachment that tend to confine and smother love. Nothing suffocates love like possessiveness. "Because you are mine, you have to do this; I have a right to treat you this way." This is often the deathblow to a human relationship.

I feel that before two persons marry, and before they have children, they should be required by law to go to a school where they would learn the art of right behavior. When one is spiritually and psychologically educated to know something about human nature and the art of getting along with others, there is then potential for a happy, harmonious, spiritually progressive family life. The soul flowers in such an enlightened relationship.

Human beings fail in their personal relationships when they cease to have respect for one another; husband for wife, wife for husband, children for parents, and parents for children. Human relationships deteriorate when friendship is lacking in them. Without friendship, the love between husband and wife, children and parents, is soon destroyed. Friendship gives the other person freedom to express himself and his own unique identity.

When there is complete understanding and communication between two souls, there is real friendship and real love. When people learn to keep friendship, respect, and regard in their marital, parental, and other relationships they will never abuse each other, or hurt themselves by such abuse.

You may say, "Yes, it would be ideal if only my husband (or wife, or children) would do it!" Why don't *you* be the one to begin it? Do your part; leave the rest in God's hands.

It always comes back to the same thing: one must begin with himself.

About the Author

Sri Daya Mata, one of Paramahansa Yogananda's earliest and closest disciples, is the president of Self-Realization Fellowship/Yogoda Satsanga Society of India.

Born Faye Wright on January 31, 1914, in Salt Lake City, Utah, Daya Mata met Paramahansa Yogananda at the age of seventeen when she attended a lecture series he was giving in her hometown. Upon hearing him speak, she inwardly thought: "This man loves God as I have always longed to love Him. He *knows* God. Him I shall follow." Not long afterward, she entered his ashram in Los Angeles as a nun of the Self-Realization Order. During more than two decades of day-to-day association with Sri Yogananda, Daya Mata served as his confidential secretary; and over the years he entrusted her with increasing spiritual and administrative responsibilities. From the beginning he singled her out for a special role, and he encouraged other disciples to pattern their lives after her example.

As Paramahansa Yogananda's spiritual successor, Sri Daya Mata has guided his society since 1955, faithfully carrying out his wishes and ideals for the dissemination of his teachings worldwide and for the establishment of Self-Realization Fellowship temples, centers, and retreats. She has made several global speaking tours, including extended visits to India. Under her leadership, the pioneering spiritual work of Paramahansa Yogananda has flourished, both in his native land and around the world. Two anthologies of her lectures and informal talks have been published, *Only Love: Living the Spiritual Life in a Changing World,* and *Finding the Joy Within You: Personal Counsel for God-Centered Living*. Many of her talks are also available on audiocassette.

A true mother of compassion as her name signifies, Sri Daya Mata has inspired truth-seekers of all faiths and from all walks of life. Dr. Binay R. Sen, former Ambassador of India to the United States, wrote in his Foreword to her second anthology: "Nowhere does Paramahansa Yogananda's legacy shine with more radiance than in his saintly disciple Sri Daya Mata, whom he prepared to carry on in his footsteps after he would be gone....Those who, like myself, were privileged to have met Paramahansaji find reflected in Daya Mataji that same spirit of divine love and compassion."

Audiocassettes of Talks by Sri Daya Mata

A Heart Aflame

Living a God-Centered Life

Let Us Be Thankful

Strengthening the Power of the Mind

Is Meditation on God Compatible With Modern Life?

Free Yourself From Tension

Understanding the Soul's Need for God

Finding God in Daily Life

Karma Yoga: Balancing Activity and Meditation

God First

Moral Courage: Effecting Positive Change Through Our Moral and Spiritual Choices

Anchoring Your Life in God

Let Every Day Be Christmas

The Way to Peace, Humility, and Love for God

"My Spirit Shall Live On...": The Final Days of Paramahansa Yogananda

Videocassette

Security in a World of Change

Paramahansa Yogananda (1893–1952)

"The ideal of love for God and service to humanity found full expression in the life of Paramahansa Yogananda....Though the major part of his life was spent outside India, still he takes his place among our great saints. His work continues to grow and shine ever more brightly, drawing people everywhere on the path of the pilgrimage of the Spirit."

—from a tribute by the Government of India upon issuing a commemorative stamp in Paramahansa Yogananda's honor

Born in India on January 5, 1893, Paramahansa Yogananda devoted his life to helping people of all races and creeds to realize and express more fully in their lives the true beauty, nobility, and divinity of the human spirit.

After graduating from Calcutta University in 1915, Sri Yogananda took formal vows as a monk of India's venerable monastic Swami Order. Two years later, he began his life's work with the founding of a "how-to-live" school—since grown to twenty-one educational institutions throughout India—where traditional academic subjects were offered together with yoga training and instruction in spiritual ideals. In 1920, he was invited to serve as India's delegate to an International Congress of Religious Liberals in Boston. His address to the Congress and subsequent lectures on the East Coast were enthusiastically received, and in 1924 he embarked on a cross-continental speaking tour.

Over the next three decades, Paramahansa Yogananda contributed in far-reaching ways to a greater awareness and appreciation in the West of the spiritual wisdom of the East. In Los Angeles, he established an international headquarters for Self-Realization Fellowship—the nonsectarian religious society he had founded in 1920. Through his writings, extensive lecture tours, and the creation of Self-Realization Fellowship temples and meditation centers, he introduced hundreds of thousands of truth-seekers to the ancient science and philosophy of Yoga and its universally applicable methods of meditation.

Today the spiritual and humanitarian work begun by Paramahansa Yogananda continues under the direction of Sri Daya Mata, one of his earliest and closest disciples and president of Self-Realization Fellowship/Yogoda Satsanga Society of India since 1955. In addition to publishing his writings, lectures, and informal talks (including a comprehensive series of *Self-Realization Fellowship Lessons* for home study), the society oversees temples, retreats, and centers around the world; the monastic communities of the Self-Realization Order; and a Worldwide Prayer Circle.

In an article on Sri Yogananda's life and work, Dr. Quincy Howe, Jr., Professor of Ancient Languages at Scripps College, wrote: "Paramahansa Yogananda brought to the West not only India's perennial promise of God-realization, but also a practical method by which spiritual aspirants from all walks of life may progress rapidly toward that goal. Originally appreciated in the West only on the most lofty and abstract level, the spiritual legacy of India is now accessible as practice and experience to all who aspire to know God, not in the beyond, but in the here and now. . . . Yogananda has placed within the reach of all the most exalted methods of contemplation."

How-to-Live Series Glossary

ashram. A spiritual hermitage; often a monastery.

astral world. The subtle world of light and energy that lies behind the physical universe. Every being, every object, every vibration on the physical plane has an astral counterpart, for in the astral universe (heaven) is the "blueprint" of the material universe. A discussion of the astral world and the still subtler causal or ideational world of thought may be found in Chapter 43 of Paramahansa Yogananda's *Autobiography of a Yogi*.

Aum (Om). The Sanskrit root word or seed-sound symbolizing that aspect of Godhead which creates and sustains all things; Cosmic Vibration. *Aum* of the Vedas became the sacred word *Hum* of the Tibetans; *Amin* of the Muslims; and *Amen* of the Egyptians, Greeks, Romans, Jews, and Christians. The world's great religions state that all created things originate in the cosmic vibratory energy of *Aum* or Amen, the Word or Holy Ghost. "In the beginning was the Word, and the Word was with God, and the Word was God.... All things were made by him [the Word or *Aum*]; and without him was not any thing made that was made" (John 1:1,3).

avatar. From the Sanskrit word *avatara* ("descent"), signifying the descent of Divinity into flesh. One who attains union with Spirit and then returns to earth to help humanity is called an avatar.

Bhagavad Gita. "Song of the Lord." Part of the ancient Indian *Mahabharata* epic, presented in the form of a dialogue between the avatar *(q.v.)* Lord Krishna and his disciple Arjuna. A profound treatise on the science of Yoga and a timeless prescription for happiness and success in everyday living.

Bhagavan Krishna (Lord Krishna). An avatar *(q.v.)* who lived in India many centuries before the Christian era. His teachings on Yoga *(q.v.)* are presented in the Bhagavad Gita. One of the meanings given for the word *Krishna* in the Hindu scriptures is "Omniscient Spirit." Thus, *Krishna,* like *Christ,* is a title signifying the spiritual magnitude of the avatar—his oneness with God. (See *Christ Consciousness.*)

Christ center. The center of concentration and will at the point between the eyebrows; seat of Christ Consciousness and of the spiritual eye *(q.v.).*

Christ Consciousness. The projected consciousness of God immanent in all creation. In Christian scripture it is called the "only begotten son," the only pure reflection in creation of God the Father; in Hindu scripture it is called *Kutastha Chaitanya,* the cosmic intelligence of Spirit everywhere present in creation. It is the universal consciousness, oneness with God, manifested by Jesus, Krishna, and other avatars. Great saints and yogis know it as the state of *samadhi (q.v.)* meditation wherein their consciousness has become identified with the intelligence in every particle of creation; they feel the entire universe as their own body.

Cosmic Consciousness. The Absolute; Spirit beyond creation. Also the *samadhi*-meditation state of oneness with God both beyond and within vibratory creation.

guru. Spiritual teacher. The *Guru Gita* (verse 17) aptly describes the guru as "dispeller of darkness" (from *gu,* "darkness" and *ru,* "that which dispels"). Though the word *guru* is often misused to refer simply to any teacher or instructor, a true God-illumined guru is one who, in his attainment of self-mastery, has realized his identity with the omnipresent Spirit. Such a one is uniquely qualified to lead others on their inward spiritual journey.

The nearest English equivalent to *guru* is the word *Master.* As a mark of respect, Paramahansa Yogananda's disciples often use this term in addressing or referring to him.

karma. The effects of past actions, from this or previous lifetimes. The law of karma is that of action and reaction, cause and effect, sowing and reaping. By their thoughts and actions, human beings become the molders of their own destinies. Whatever energies a person has set into motion, wisely or unwisely, must return to that person as their starting point, like a circle inexorably completing itself. An individual's karma follows him or her from incarnation to incarnation until fulfilled or spiritually transcended. (See *reincarnation.*)

Krishna. See *Bhagavan Krishna.*

Kriya Yoga. A sacred spiritual science, originating millenniums ago in India. A form of *Raja* ("royal" or "complete") *Yoga,* it includes certain advanced techniques of meditation that lead to direct, personal experience of God. *Kriya Yoga* is explained in Chapter 26 of *Autobiography of a Yogi,* and is taught to students of the *Self-Realization Fellowship Lessons* who fulfill certain spiritual requirements.

maya. The delusory power inherent in the structure of creation, by which the One appears as many. *Maya* is the principle of relativity, inversion, contrast, duality, oppositional states; the "Satan" (lit., in Hebrew, "the adversary") of the Old Testament prophets. Paramahansa Yogananda wrote: "The Sanskrit word *maya* means 'the measurer'; it is the magical power in creation by which limitations and divisions are apparently present in the Immeasurable and Inseparable....In God's plan and play *(lila),* the sole function of Satan or *maya* is to attempt to divert man from Spirit to matter, from Reality to unreality....*Maya* is the veil of transitoriness in Nature...the veil that each man must lift in order to see behind it the Creator, the changeless Immutable, eternal Reality."

paramahansa. A spiritual title signifying one who has attained the highest state of unbroken communion with God. It may be conferred only by a true guru on a qualified disciple. Swami Sri Yukteswar bestowed the title on Paramahansa Yogananda in 1935.

reincarnation. A discussion of reincarnation may be found in Chapter 43 of Paramahansa Yogananda's *Autobiography of a Yogi*. As explained there, by the law of karma *(q.v.),* the past actions of human beings set into motion the effects that draw them back to this material plane. Through a succession of births and deaths they return to earth repeatedly to undergo here the experiences that are the fruits of those past actions, and to continue a process of spiritual evolution that leads ultimately to realization of the soul's inherent perfection and union with God.

samadhi. Spiritual ecstasy; superconscious experience; ultimately, union with God as the all-pervading supreme Reality.

Satan. See *maya*.

Self. Capitalized to denote the *atman,* or soul, the divine essence of man, as distinguished from the ordinary self, which is the human personality or ego. The Self is individualized Spirit, whose essential nature is ever-existing, ever-conscious, ever-new Bliss.

Self-realization. Realization of one's true identity as the Self, one with the universal consciousness of God. Paramahansa Yogananda wrote: "Self-realization is the knowing—in body, mind, and soul—that we are one with the omnipresence of God; that we do not have to pray that it come to us, that we are not merely near it at all times, but that God's omnipresence is our omnipresence; that we are just as much a part of Him now as we ever will be. All we have to do is improve our knowing."

spiritual eye. The single eye of intuition and spiritual perception at the Christ *(Kutastha)* center *(q.v.)* between the eyebrows; the entryway into higher states of consciousness. During deep meditation, the single or spiritual eye becomes visible as a bright star surrounded by a sphere of blue light that, in turn, is encircled by a brilliant halo of golden light. This omniscient eye is variously referred to in scriptures as the third eye, the star of the East, the inner eye, the dove descending from heaven, the eye of Shiva, and the eye of intuition. "If therefore thine eye be single, thy whole body shall be full of light" (Matthew 6:22).

Yoga. The word *Yoga* (from the Sanskrit *yuj,* "union") means union of the individual soul with Spirit; also, the methods by which this goal is attained. There are various systems of Yoga. That taught by Paramahansa Yogananda is *Raja Yoga,* the "royal" or "complete" yoga, which centers around practice of scientific methods of meditation. The sage Patanjali, foremost ancient exponent of Yoga, has outlined eight definite steps by which the *Raja Yogi* attains *samadhi,* or union with God. These are (1) *yama,* moral conduct; (2) *niyama,* religious observances; (3) *asana,* right posture to still bodily restlessness; (4) *pranayama,* control of *prana,* subtle life currents; (5) *pratyahara,* interiorization; (6) *dharana,* concentration; (7) *dhyana,* meditation; and (8) *samadhi,* superconscious experience.

BOOKS BY PARAMAHANSA YOGANANDA

Available at bookstores or directly from the publisher:

SELF-REALIZATION FELLOWSHIP
3880 San Rafael Avenue • Los Angeles, CA 90065-3298
Tel (213) 225-2471 Fax (213) 225-5088

Autobiography of a Yogi

Man's Eternal Quest

The Divine Romance

The Science of Religion

Wine of the Mystic: *The Rubaiyat of Omar Khayyam—A Spiritual Interpretation*

Where There Is Light: *Insight and Inspiration for Meeting Life's Challenges*

Whispers from Eternity

Songs of the Soul

Sayings of Paramahansa Yogananda

Scientific Healing Affirmations

How You Can Talk With God

Metaphysical Meditations

The Law of Success

Cosmic Chants

A complete catalog of books and audio/video recordings is available on request.

Free Introductory Booklet

Undreamed-of Possibilities provides an introduction to the teachings of Paramahansa Yogananda and the scientific techniques of meditation he taught, including Kriya Yoga. This booklet also explains how one may receive the *Self-Realization Fellowship Lessons,* which offer instruction in these techniques.

Other Titles in the "How-to-Live" Series

Paramahansa Yogananda

Answered Prayers

Focusing the Power of Attention for Success

Harmonizing Physical, Mental, and Spiritual Methods of Healing

Healing by God's Unlimited Power

How to Cultivate Divine Love

How to Find a Way to Victory

Remolding Your Life

Ridding the Consciousness of Worry

Where Are Our Departed Loved Ones?

World Crisis

Sri Daya Mata

Overcoming Character Liabilities

The Skilled Profession of Child-Rearing

Mrinalini Mata

The Guru-Disciple Relationship

Brother Anandamoy

Closing the Generation Gap

Spiritual Marriage

Brother Bhaktananda

Applying the Power of Positive Thinking

Brother Premamoy

Bringing Out the Best in Our Relationships With Others

Autobiography of a Yogi
by Paramahansa Yogananda

This acclaimed autobiography presents a fascinating portrait of one of the great spiritual figures of our time. With engaging candor, eloquence, and wit, Paramahansa Yogananda narrates the inspiring chronicle of his life—the experiences of his remarkable childhood, encounters with many saints and sages during his youthful search throughout India for an illumined teacher, ten years of training in the hermitage of a revered yoga master, and the thirty years that he lived and taught in America. Also recorded here are his meetings with Mahatma Gandhi, Rabindranath Tagore, Luther Burbank, the Catholic stigmatist Therese Neumann, and other celebrated spiritual personalities of East and West.

Autobiography of a Yogi is at once a beautifully written account of an exceptional life and a profound introduction to the ancient science of Yoga and its time-honored tradition of meditation. The author clearly explains the subtle but definite laws behind both the ordinary events of everyday life and the extraordinary events commonly termed miracles. His absorbing life story thus becomes the background for a penetrating and unforgettable look at the ultimate mysteries of human existence.

Considered a modern spiritual classic, the book has been translated into eighteen languages and is widely used as a text and reference work in colleges and universities. A perennial best-seller since it was first published nearly fifty years ago, *Autobiography of a Yogi* has found its way into the hearts of millions of readers around the world.

"A rare account."—The New York Times

"A fascinating and clearly annotated study."
—Newsweek

"There has been nothing before, written in English or in any other European language, like this presentation of Yoga."
—Columbia University Press